The David Tepper Story Of Resilience and Wealth

From Steel City Roots to Wall Street Supremacy: The Visionary Strategies and Billion-Dollar Gambles That Transformed a Pittsburgh Kid into a Hedge Fund Icon

Victor C. Hopkins

Copyright © Victor C. Hopkins

2024

All rights reserved, No part of this publication may be reproduced, distributed, or transmitted in any form or by any means, including photocopying, recording, or other electronic or mechanical methods, without the prior written permission of the publisher, except in the case of brief quotations embodied in critical reviews and certain other noncommercial uses permitted by copyright law.

Table of Contents

Introduction
David Tepper's Journey: From Steel City to Wall Street Titan

Chapter One; Early Life and Education
Childhood in Pittsburgh, Pennsylvania
Influence of Family and Early Lessons in Work Ethic
High School Achievements and Extracurricular Activities
Education at the University of Pittsburgh: Undergraduate Experiences and Challenges
MBA from Carnegie Mellon University: Significant Academic Achievements and Early Insights into Finance

Chapter Two; Early Career and Wall Street Ascent

First Roles at Republic Steel and Keystone Mutual Funds: Key Learning Experiences
Joining Goldman Sachs: Tepper's Rapid Rise and Notable Contributions
Managing Through the 1987 Stock Market Crash: Strategies and Impact
Leaving Goldman Sachs: Reasons and Reflections on Career Moves

Chapter Three; Founding Appaloosa Management
The Vision Behind Appaloosa Management's Inception in 1993
Early Challenges and Overcoming Skepticism in the Hedge Fund Industry
Initial Successes and Tepper's Distinct Investment Approach
Development of Investment Philosophy: Contrarian Bets and Risk Management
Chapter Four; Appaloosa's Biggest Wins

Tepper's Contrarian Strategies During the 2008 Financial Crisis: Details of Key Trades
Major Profits from Distressed Debt Investments: GM, Chrysler, and Others
Other Significant Investments That Contributed to Appaloosa's Success
Analysis of Tepper's Risk-Taking and Market Insights

Chapter Five; Philanthropy and Ownership of Sports Teams
Tepper's Philanthropic Endeavors: Major Donations and Causes Supported
Contributions to Carnegie Mellon University and Other Institutions
Acquisition of the Carolina Panthers NFL Team: Motivations and Impact
Launching Charlotte FC MLS Team: Vision and Objectives

Tepper's Broader Goals with Sports Team Ownership and Community Engagement
Enhancing Community Engagement Through Sports
Driving Economic Development Through Sports Investments
Promoting Diversity and Inclusion in Sports
Long-Term Vision and Impact of Tepper's Philanthropy and Sports Investments

Chapter Six; Tepper's Leadership and Management Style
Analysis of Tepper's Leadership Qualities and Decision-Making Processes
Unconventional Methods: Examples of His Unorthodox Approach to Business
Focus on Talent, Intelligence, and Risk-Taking Over Traditional Experience

Insights from Colleagues and Employees on Working with Tepper
Driving Innovation and Success at Appaloosa Management
Building a Culture of Excellence and Accountability

Chapter Seven; Tepper's Wealth and Lifestyle
Overview of Tepper's Net Worth and Standing Among Global Billionaires
Tepper's Personal Investments in Real Estate, Cars, and Art
Reflection on Tepper's Lifestyle Choices and Public Image as a "Regular Guy"

Conclusion

Introduction

David Tepper's Journey: From Steel City to Wall Street Titan

David Tepper's story is the quintessential American dream - a tale of grit, intelligence, and unconventional thinking that has propelled him from humble beginnings in the steel city of Pittsburgh to the rarefied heights of billionaire status.

Tepper's journey is a captivating odyssey that inspires and enlightens, showcasing the transformative power of relentless ambition, unwavering discipline, and a willingness to challenge the status quo. Born in 1957 to a middle-class Jewish family, Tepper's early years were marked by a deep fascination with finance and a proclivity for risk-taking that would foreshadow his remarkable career. As a young boy, he avidly collected baseball cards and honed his skills in stock trading, demonstrating an innate talent for identifying undervalued opportunities and capitalizing on them.

This innate drive and analytical prowess would become the hallmarks of Tepper's approach to the world of finance.

From Steel City to Wall Street
Tepper's path to success was paved with a relentless pursuit of knowledge and a willingness to take calculated risks. After earning a degree in economics from the University of Pittsburgh, he went on to obtain a master's in industrial administration from the prestigious Carnegie Mellon University, honing his skills in finance and investment strategy.

Armed with this formidable academic foundation, Tepper embarked on a journey that would ultimately transform him into one of the most influential figures in the world of hedge funds. Tepper's early career was marked by a series of pivotal experiences that would shape his approach to the financial markets. His stint at Republic Steel and Keystone Mutual Funds provided him with invaluable insights into the distressed company sector, a domain that would later become a cornerstone of his investment philosophy. However, it was his time at Goldman Sachs that truly ignited Tepper's meteoric rise. As a credit analyst and head trader, he played a crucial role in ensuring the firm's survival during the tumultuous 1987 stock market crash, solidifying his reputation as a savvy and resilient operator.

Founding Appaloosa Management
Despite his success at Goldman Sachs, Tepper's ambition and unconventional thinking led him to take a bold leap in 1993, when he founded his own hedge fund, Appaloosa Management. In the face of skepticism and naysayers, Tepper built Appaloosa from the ground up, leveraging his deep understanding of distressed debt and his unwavering conviction in his investment strategies. Appaloosa's early years were marked by remarkable success,

with the fund delivering net returns of 57.6% in the second half of 1993 and growing its assets to $800 million by 1996. Tepper's expertise in navigating the complexities of distressed debt, both for nations and companies, became a hallmark of his investment approach. His prescient bets during the 1997 Korean currency crisis and his savvy investments in the debt of utilities like Williams Companies in the early 2000s further cemented his reputation as a financial maverick.

Tepper's journey, however, was not without its challenges. Appaloosa experienced significant volatility, with losses of 29% in 1998 during the Russian default and 27% during the 2008 financial crisis. But Tepper's resilience and adaptability shone through, as he consistently found ways to bounce back and capitalize on market opportunities. His ability to identify undervalued assets and his willingness to take bold, contrarian positions became the hallmarks of his investment strategy. One of Tepper's most remarkable achievements came during the 2008 financial crisis, when he made a series of prescient bets on the distressed debt of automakers like General Motors and Chrysler. His unwavering conviction and his ability to see beyond the prevailing gloom allowed him to reap massive profits, cementing his status as one of the most successful hedge fund managers of the era.

Tepper's success has not only transformed his own life but has also had a profound impact on the communities he has touched. His philanthropic efforts, including a $55 million donation to Carnegie Mellon University and significant contributions to education reform and hurricane relief efforts, have left an indelible mark on the world. In recent years, Tepper has also made a foray into the world of professional sports, purchasing the Carolina Panthers NFL team in 2018 for a record-breaking

$2.3 billion. This move not only showcases his business acumen but also his passion for sports and his desire to leave a lasting legacy. David Tepper's journey from the steel city of Pittsburgh to the pinnacles of Wall Street is a testament to the power of unwavering determination, intellectual curiosity, and a willingness to challenge conventional wisdom.

His story inspires and captivates, reminding us that with grit, intelligence, and a relentless pursuit of excellence, even the most daunting of dreams can be realized.
As Tepper continues to shape the world of finance and philanthropy, his legacy will undoubtedly endure, serving as a shining example of the transformative potential of the American dream. His story is a testament to the enduring power of the human spirit, a reminder that with the right mindset and the courage to take calculated risks, even the most humble of beginnings can give rise to extraordinary achievements.

Chapter One; Early Life and Education

David Tepper's trajectory from a humble upbringing to a towering figure in finance and sports ownership is a testament to the transformative power of resilience, education, and strategic risk-taking. His early life and education laid the critical groundwork for his later achievements, shaping his values, perspectives, and the audacious approach he would bring to the financial world.

Childhood in Pittsburgh, Pennsylvania

David Tepper was born on September 11, 1957, in the modest environment of Pittsburgh, Pennsylvania. Pittsburgh, historically a robust steel town, was in a state of economic flux during Tepper's formative years. The industrial backdrop of the city, characterized by its blue-collar ethos, deeply influenced Tepper's upbringing. His father, Harry Tepper, worked as an accountant, while his mother,

Roberta Tepper, was an elementary school teacher. Their professions instilled in David a respect for hard work and education from a young age.

The Teppers resided in a typical working-class neighborhood, where David witnessed firsthand the importance of perseverance and determination. The values imbibed from his family's daily struggles and triumphs would later serve as a bedrock for his tenacious character. His father's meticulousness with numbers and his mother's dedication to teaching offered contrasting yet complementary influences that shaped his analytical mindset and value for learning.

Influence of Family and Early Lessons in Work Ethic

David Tepper's parents emphasized the importance of education and a strong work ethic. His father, despite the challenges of raising a family on an accountant's salary, managed to provide for his children and instill in them a disciplined approach to life.

Harry Tepper's financial acumen and diligent work habits were not lost on young David, who often saw his father meticulously managing the family's finances and discussing economic matters. Roberta Tepper, on the other hand, contributed to David's development through her passion for education. Her career as a teacher made her an advocate for lifelong learning, encouraging David to value his studies and strive for academic excellence. Roberta's nurturing nature, combined with her insistence on intellectual curiosity, played a crucial role in fostering David's early interest in numbers and problem-solving. These familial influences were not just about instilling values but also about providing a support system that encouraged David to pursue his interests. This environment cultivated a sense of self-reliance and the belief that hard work could transcend socioeconomic limitations, a philosophy that would become a cornerstone of Tepper's career.

High School Achievements and Extracurricular Activities

David Tepper attended Peabody High School in Pittsburgh, where his aptitude for academics and extracurricular involvement began to surface prominently. Known for his prowess in mathematics, Tepper quickly distinguished himself as a student with a keen analytical mind. His high school years were marked by an intense curiosity and a drive to excel, characteristics that set him apart from his peers.

In addition to his academic pursuits, Tepper was actively involved in various extracurricular activities. He participated in the school's debate team, honing his skills in critical thinking and public speaking. These activities not only augmented his intellectual abilities but also provided him with early experiences in leadership and collaboration.

His involvement in sports, particularly baseball, further developed his competitive spirit and understanding of teamwork. Tepper's high school years were crucial in shaping his character. The challenges he faced in balancing academic demands with extracurricular activities taught him the importance of time management and perseverance. These experiences laid the groundwork for the disciplined and strategic mindset that would later characterize his approach to business and investing.

Education at the University of Pittsburgh: Undergraduate Experiences and Challenges

After graduating from high school, Tepper enrolled at the University of Pittsburgh. His choice to stay close to home reflected his pragmatic approach to education and his desire to remain connected to his roots. At Pitt, Tepper pursued a degree in economics, a field that would provide him with the foundational knowledge necessary for his future endeavors in finance.

The university years were a time of significant personal and academic growth for Tepper. He immersed himself in his studies, developing a deep understanding of economic principles and their practical applications. His professors noted his exceptional analytical skills and his ability to grasp complex concepts quickly. Tepper's coursework in economics and finance helped him build a robust intellectual framework that would later inform his investment strategies. While excelling academically, Tepper also had to navigate the typical challenges of college life. He worked various part-time jobs to support himself, demonstrating the work ethic instilled by his parents.

These jobs ranged from delivering pizzas to working in the university's library, experiences that reinforced his understanding of the value of hard work and financial independence. Tepper's undergraduate years were also marked by his burgeoning interest in the stock market. He began investing modest amounts of his savings, experimenting with different strategies and gaining firsthand experience in trading. These early forays into investing provided him with practical insights and solidified his passion for finance.

MBA from Carnegie Mellon University: Significant Academic Achievements and Early Insights into Finance

After completing his undergraduate degree, Tepper pursued an MBA at Carnegie Mellon University's Tepper School of Business (which would later be named in his honor following his substantial donations). This decision marked a pivotal point in his academic and professional journey, as it provided him with the advanced knowledge and skills necessary to excel in the competitive world of finance.

At Carnegie Mellon, Tepper was exposed to a rigorous academic environment that challenged him to refine his analytical and quantitative abilities. The MBA program emphasized data-driven decision-making and innovative financial strategies, aligning perfectly with Tepper's intellectual inclinations. He excelled in his coursework, particularly in subjects related to financial analysis, investment management, and economic theory. One of the most significant aspects of Tepper's MBA experience was the opportunity to learn from leading experts in the field. His professors, many of whom were renowned economists and financial analysts, provided him with invaluable insights into the complexities of the global financial markets.

These interactions helped Tepper develop a nuanced understanding of market dynamics and the interplay between economic policies and financial instruments. During his time at Carnegie Mellon, Tepper also participated in various case competitions and finance-related projects. These experiences allowed him to apply his theoretical knowledge to real-world scenarios, further honing his problem-solving skills. His performance in these activities earned him recognition among his peers and faculty, solidifying his reputation as a promising young financier.

Tepper's MBA years were not solely defined by academic achievements. He continued to engage in practical investing, managing a small portfolio that included stocks, bonds, and other financial instruments. This hands-on experience complemented his formal education, providing him with a deeper understanding of market behavior and investment strategies.

Moreover, Tepper's time at Carnegie Mellon was instrumental in shaping his approach to risk management. The rigorous coursework and practical projects emphasized the importance of balancing risk and reward, a principle that would become a hallmark of Tepper's investment philosophy. He learned to analyze financial data meticulously, anticipate market trends, and make informed decisions based on a combination of empirical evidence and intuitive judgment.

David Tepper's early life and education played a crucial role in shaping the man who would become one of the most successful hedge fund managers and philanthropists of his generation. His childhood in Pittsburgh instilled in him a strong work ethic and a deep respect for education.

His academic achievements, particularly his MBA from Carnegie Mellon University, equipped him with the knowledge and skills necessary to navigate the complexities of the financial markets. These formative experiences, coupled with his innate curiosity and drive, laid the foundation for a remarkable career characterized by strategic brilliance and an unwavering commitment to excellence. Tepper's journey from Pittsburgh's working-class neighborhoods to the pinnacle of the financial world is a testament to the transformative power of education and perseverance.

Chapter Two; Early Career and Wall Street Ascent

David Tepper's rise in the world of finance began with a series of strategic career moves and learning experiences that gradually built his reputation as a shrewd investor. His early roles at Republic Steel and Keystone Mutual Funds, his pivotal tenure at Goldman Sachs, and his deft navigation of the 1987 stock market crash were all crucial in shaping his professional trajectory and approach to investing. Each step in Tepper's early career contributed to his eventual success as a leading figure on Wall Street.

First Roles at Republic Steel and Keystone Mutual Funds: Key Learning Experiences

David Tepper's entry into the professional world began at Republic Steel, a prominent company in the steel industry. After completing his MBA at Carnegie Mellon University, Tepper joined Republic Steel as a credit analyst. This role, though not directly related to his later focus on finance, provided him with valuable insights into corporate operations, financial analysis, and risk management. At Republic Steel, Tepper was responsible for assessing the creditworthiness of various clients and projects.

This required a thorough understanding of financial statements, cash flow analysis, and economic conditions. His analytical skills were put to the test as he evaluated the financial health of the company's clients, learning to identify potential risks and opportunities. This experience honed Tepper's ability to scrutinize financial data and make informed decisions, skills that would prove indispensable in his future roles. Following his stint at Republic Steel, Tepper transitioned to Keystone Mutual Funds. This move marked his first significant step into the financial sector. At Keystone, Tepper worked as a credit analyst and a bond analyst, focusing on fixed-income securities.

His responsibilities included evaluating the credit risk of various bond issuers, analyzing market trends, and making recommendations on bond investments.

Working at Keystone Mutual Funds gave Tepper a deeper understanding of the bond market and fixed-income securities, which are critical components of the financial industry. This role broadened his perspective on investment strategies and financial markets, providing him with practical experience in asset management and investment analysis. Tepper's work at Keystone also exposed him to the complexities of portfolio management and the intricacies of balancing risk and return, further refining his investment philosophy.

Joining Goldman Sachs: Tepper's Rapid Rise and Notable Contributions

David Tepper's career took a significant turn when he joined Goldman Sachs in 1985. At Goldman, Tepper initially worked as a credit analyst in the risk arbitrage department, a role that quickly propelled him into the spotlight due to his exceptional analytical abilities and keen insights into market dynamics.

Goldman Sachs, a leading investment bank, offered Tepper a platform to demonstrate his talents in a highly competitive environment. His early responsibilities involved assessing merger and acquisition deals, analyzing their financial implications, and identifying arbitrage opportunities. Tepper's knack for identifying undervalued assets and his meticulous approach to financial analysis soon earned him a reputation as a rising star within the firm.

Tepper's ascent at Goldman Sachs was rapid. Recognizing his potential, the firm promoted him to head trader within the high-yield trading desk. In this role, Tepper managed significant portfolios of high-yield bonds, focusing on distressed debt and complex securities. His responsibilities included making investment decisions, executing trades, and managing risks associated with high-yield securities.

One of Tepper's notable contributions during his tenure at Goldman Sachs was his ability to navigate the turbulent high-yield bond market. His deep understanding of credit risk and market trends allowed him to make informed decisions that often yielded substantial profits for the firm. Tepper's strategic approach to distressed debt investing involved identifying companies that were undervalued due to financial distress but had the potential for recovery. By investing in these companies' bonds at discounted prices, Tepper was able to capitalize on their eventual turnaround, generating significant returns. Tepper's success in the high-yield trading desk solidified his reputation as a talented trader with an exceptional ability to identify and exploit market inefficiencies. His contributions to Goldman Sachs during this period were instrumental in enhancing the firm's profitability and establishing its dominance in the high-yield bond market.

Managing Through the 1987 Stock Market Crash: Strategies and Impact

The 1987 stock market crash, often referred to as "Black Monday," was a critical test of David Tepper's skills and resilience. On October 19, 1987, global stock markets experienced a sudden and severe decline, with the Dow Jones Industrial Average plummeting by 22.6% in a single day. This unprecedented market collapse sent shockwaves through the financial industry, causing widespread panic and uncertainty.

At the time of the crash, Tepper was entrenched in his role as a head trader at Goldman Sachs, responsible for managing high-yield bond portfolios. The market turmoil posed significant challenges, particularly for those dealing with high-risk securities like the ones Tepper handled.

However, Tepper's strategic acumen and composure under pressure allowed him to navigate the crisis effectively. Tepper's approach to managing through the crash involved a combination of risk mitigation and opportunistic investing. Anticipating potential market instability, Tepper had previously implemented risk management strategies to safeguard his portfolios. These strategies included diversifying investments, maintaining adequate liquidity, and closely monitoring market indicators. His preparedness enabled him to respond swiftly to the market downturn, minimizing losses and preserving capital during the initial phase of the crash.

In the aftermath of the crash, Tepper identified opportunities in the distressed debt market. Many companies faced financial difficulties due to the market collapse, leading to a surge in distressed debt securities. Tepper's expertise in analyzing credit risk and distressed assets positioned him to capitalize on these opportunities.

He selectively invested in distressed bonds of companies that, despite their immediate challenges, had strong underlying fundamentals and the potential for recovery. Tepper's ability to navigate the 1987 stock market crash not only mitigated losses for Goldman Sachs but also demonstrated his proficiency in managing high-stress situations and turning issues into opportunities.

His performance during this tumultuous period further cemented his reputation as a capable and strategic investor, earning him accolades within the firm and the broader financial community.

Leaving Goldman Sachs: Reasons and Reflections on Career Moves

Despite his success at Goldman Sachs, David Tepper made the pivotal decision to leave the firm in 1992. His departure was motivated by a combination of personal ambition, professional aspirations, and a desire for greater autonomy in his investment decisions.

One of the primary reasons for Tepper's departure was his frustration with the firm's partnership structure and internal politics. Despite his significant contributions to the high-yield trading desk, Tepper felt that his career progression was being stymied by the firm's conservative approach to promotions and its rigid hierarchical structure. He believed that his potential and contributions warranted a more prominent role, but the firm's decision-making processes did not align with his aspirations for rapid advancement.

Additionally, Tepper's entrepreneurial spirit and desire for independence played a crucial role in his decision to leave Goldman Sachs. He had developed a clear vision for his own investment strategies and approaches, which he felt could be more effectively executed in an independent setting. Tepper wanted the freedom to make bold investment decisions without the constraints imposed by a large corporate entity.

This desire for autonomy and control over his professional destiny led him to consider establishing his own hedge fund. Reflecting on his career moves, Tepper viewed his departure from Goldman Sachs as a necessary step towards realizing his full potential. He recognized that his experiences at Goldman had equipped him with invaluable skills, knowledge, and industry connections, but he also understood that his future growth depended on his ability to operate independently and implement his own investment philosophies. Shortly after leaving Goldman Sachs, Tepper founded Appaloosa Management in 1993. This new venture allowed him to leverage his expertise in high-yield bonds and distressed debt investing, applying the strategies and insights he had developed throughout his career.

The establishment of Appaloosa Management marked the beginning of a new chapter in Tepper's professional journey, where he could fully harness his talents and pursue his vision of strategic investing. David Tepper's early career and ascent on Wall Street were characterized by a series of strategic decisions, key learning experiences, and notable contributions to the financial industry. His roles at Republic Steel and Keystone Mutual Funds provided him with a solid foundation in financial analysis and risk management. His tenure at Goldman Sachs showcased his exceptional skills in high-yield bond trading and his ability to navigate complex market conditions, particularly during the 1987 stock market crash. Tepper's decision to leave Goldman Sachs, driven by his desire for greater autonomy and control over his investment strategies, ultimately paved the way for the founding of Appaloosa Management and his subsequent success as a leading hedge fund manager. Each step in Tepper's early career was instrumental in shaping his approach to investing and establishing his legacy in the world of finance.

Chapter Three; Founding Appaloosa Management

David Tepper's decision to establish Appaloosa Management in 1993 marked a turning point in his career and the hedge fund industry. Armed with a wealth of experience from his tenure at Goldman Sachs and an acute understanding of distressed debt, Tepper envisioned a firm that could capitalize on contrarian investment strategies. Appaloosa Management quickly distinguished itself through its bold approach to risk and an uncanny ability to navigate financial turbulence.

The Vision Behind Appaloosa Management's Inception in 1993

The early 1990s were a period of substantial transformation in the financial markets. The recession of the early 1990s, coupled with the aftermath of the 1987 stock market crash, created a landscape ripe for innovative investment strategies.

David Tepper, having just departed Goldman Sachs, saw an opportunity to leverage his expertise in high-yield bonds and distressed debt in a new venture.

Tepper's vision for Appaloosa Management was grounded in the belief that significant returns could be achieved by investing in distressed assets during times of economic uncertainty. He identified a niche where traditional investment firms were either hesitant or unable to tread—buying the debt of troubled companies at a discount and profiting from their recovery. This contrarian approach, focusing on undervalued or out-of-favor securities, was the cornerstone of Tepper's investment philosophy. Appaloosa Management was conceived as a hedge fund that would thrive on volatility and market dislocations. Tepper's goal was to build a firm that could navigate economic downturns and financial crises by identifying opportunities where others saw only risk.

He believed that by applying rigorous analysis and maintaining a disciplined approach to risk management, Appaloosa could generate substantial returns for its investors while mitigating potential downsides.

Early Challenges and Overcoming Skepticism in the Hedge Fund Industry

The founding of Appaloosa Management was not without its challenges. In the early 1990s, the hedge fund industry was still relatively nascent and often viewed with skepticism by traditional investors. Raising capital for a new fund, particularly one focused on distressed debt, was a formidable task.

Many potential investors were wary of the risks associated with high-yield securities and doubted the viability of Tepper's contrarian investment strategy. Despite these hurdles, Tepper's track record at Goldman Sachs provided him with a degree of credibility. His success in managing high-yield bonds and his ability to navigate the 1987 stock market crash were compelling arguments in favor of his new venture. Tepper leveraged his network of contacts in the financial industry to attract initial investors, emphasizing his expertise and the unique opportunities offered by Appaloosa's investment approach. Appaloosa's early days were marked by a period of intense scrutiny and skepticism. Many industry observers doubted that a small, newly established hedge fund could compete with larger, more established firms.

Additionally, Tepper faced operational challenges, including building a team, establishing infrastructure, and developing robust risk management processes. However, Tepper's perseverance and belief in his investment philosophy began to pay off. He carefully selected a team of professionals who shared his vision and possessed the analytical skills necessary to evaluate distressed assets. Appaloosa's lean and agile structure allowed it to respond quickly to market opportunities and manage its investments with precision.

Initial Successes and Tepper's Distinct Investment Approach

Appaloosa Management's initial successes can be attributed to Tepper's distinct investment approach and his ability to capitalize on market inefficiencies. The firm's strategy of investing in distressed debt during periods of economic instability allowed it to acquire undervalued assets at significant discounts.

As the economy recovered and companies stabilized, these investments often appreciated in value, generating substantial returns for the fund. One of the early successes for Appaloosa was its investment in the distressed debt of steel companies during the early 1990s. The steel industry was struggling with overcapacity and financial distress, leading to a significant decline in the value of its bonds. Tepper, recognizing the long-term potential of these companies despite their current challenges, invested heavily in their debt. As the industry began to recover, the value of these bonds increased, resulting in significant profits for Appaloosa.

Another notable success was Appaloosa's investment in the distressed debt of emerging markets during the financial crises of the 1990s. The Mexican Peso Crisis of 1994 and the Asian Financial Crisis of 1997 created opportunities to buy the debt of emerging market companies at steep discounts. Tepper's contrarian approach, combined with his ability to analyze the underlying fundamentals of these economies, allowed Appaloosa to make profitable investments during these periods of turmoil. Tepper's distinct investment approach was characterized by his willingness to take calculated risks and his ability to remain steadfast in his convictions. He often invested in assets that were shunned by traditional investors due to perceived risks or short-term challenges.

Tepper's deep understanding of market dynamics and his ability to conduct thorough due diligence enabled him to identify opportunities where others saw only danger. This contrarian mindset became a defining feature of Appaloosa's investment strategy.

Development of Investment Philosophy: Contrarian Bets and Risk Management

David Tepper's investment philosophy at Appaloosa Management was built around the principles of contrarian investing and rigorous risk management. His approach involved buying undervalued or distressed assets during times of market dislocation and holding them until their true value was realized.

This philosophy required a combination of analytical acumen, patience, and a strong stomach for volatility. A key element of Tepper's contrarian approach was his focus on distressed debt. Unlike equity investors, who often shied away from companies in financial distress, Tepper saw value in their debt securities. He believed that by purchasing these bonds at a discount, he could benefit from both the interest payments and the potential for capital appreciation as the companies recovered. This strategy required a deep understanding of the companies' financials and the broader economic environment, as well as a willingness to invest when others were selling.

Tepper's success in distressed debt investing was underpinned by his meticulous research and due diligence. He and his team at Appaloosa conducted exhaustive analyses of potential investments, examining everything from financial statements and management teams to industry trends and macroeconomic factors. This thorough approach enabled them to identify assets with strong recovery potential and avoid those with insurmountable challenges. Risk management was another critical component of Appaloosa's investment philosophy. Tepper understood that investing in distressed assets carried inherent risks, including the possibility of default or prolonged financial difficulties.

To mitigate these risks, Appaloosa employed a variety of strategies, including diversification, liquidity management, and careful position sizing. By spreading investments across multiple distressed assets and maintaining adequate liquidity, the firm was able to manage its risk exposure and preserve capital during periods of market volatility.

Tepper's approach to risk management also involved a keen awareness of market timing. He recognized that the best opportunities often arose during times of market panic or economic uncertainty. By maintaining a contrarian stance and being prepared to invest when others were retreating, Appaloosa was able to capitalize on market dislocations and generate outsized returns. This approach required not only analytical skills but also the psychological resilience to withstand market pressure and remain committed to his investment thesis.

Over time, Tepper's investment philosophy evolved to incorporate a broader range of assets and strategies. While distressed debt remained a core focus, Appaloosa also began to invest in equities, real estate, and other alternative assets. This diversification allowed the firm to capitalize on a wider array of opportunities and adapt to changing market conditions.

Despite this expansion, the principles of contrarian investing and rigorous risk management continued to guide Appaloosa's strategy. The founding of Appaloosa Management was a pivotal moment in David Tepper's career and a significant development in the hedge fund industry. Tepper's vision of a firm that thrived on market volatility and invested in distressed assets proved to be both innovative and highly successful. Despite early challenges and skepticism, Appaloosa quickly established itself as a leading hedge fund, known for its bold investment approach and exceptional returns. Tepper's distinct investment philosophy, characterized by contrarian bets and rigorous risk management, was instrumental in Appaloosa's success. His ability to identify undervalued assets, conduct thorough research, and manage risk effectively set the firm apart from its competitors.

As Appaloosa Management grew, it continued to adhere to these principles, navigating economic downturns and market dislocations with remarkable agility. Today, Appaloosa Management stands as a testament to the power of contrarian investing and the importance of disciplined risk management. David Tepper's journey from Wall Street trader to hedge fund titan is a compelling story of innovation, resilience, and strategic acumen.

His legacy at Appaloosa is a reflection of his unwavering commitment to finding value where others see only risk and his ability to turn market adversity into opportunity.

Chapter Four; Appaloosa's Biggest Wins

Appaloosa Management's rise to prominence in the hedge fund industry can be attributed to a series of strategic investments and a keen ability to navigate market turmoil. Under David Tepper's leadership, the firm capitalized on distressed debt opportunities and leveraged contrarian strategies to achieve remarkable success.

The financial crisis of 2008, along with key investments in companies like GM and Chrysler, showcased Tepper's acumen for identifying undervalued assets and executing profitable trades in high-risk environments. This chapter delves into Appaloosa's most significant wins, detailing the strategies, trades, and market insights that defined its success.

Tepper's Contrarian Strategies During the 2008 Financial Crisis: Details of Key Trades

The 2008 financial crisis, marked by the collapse of major financial institutions and a severe economic downturn, presented a defining moment for Appaloosa Management. While many investors were retreating in the face of plummeting asset prices and unprecedented market volatility, David Tepper saw an opportunity to apply his contrarian investment philosophy on a grand scale.

As the crisis unfolded, Tepper recognized that the panic-induced sell-off had created a plethora of undervalued assets, particularly in the financial sector. His strategy centered around identifying securities that were unfairly punished by the market's fear and uncertainty. Tepper's analysis led him to focus on the debt and equity of financial institutions that were facing severe liquidity issues but possessed strong underlying fundamentals. One of Tepper's most notable moves during the crisis was his investment in the preferred shares and bonds of major banks, including Citigroup and Bank of America. In late 2008 and early 2009, these financial giants were grappling with massive losses and the threat of insolvency.

Their stocks and bonds were trading at historically low prices, reflecting widespread pessimism about their survival. Tepper, however, believed that these institutions were "too big to fail" and that the government would step in to stabilize them. Tepper's bet hinged on the assumption that the federal government's intervention, through programs like the Troubled Asset Relief Program (TARP), would provide the necessary capital and liquidity to keep these banks afloat. His investment thesis was validated as the government injected billions of dollars into the financial system, leading to a recovery in the prices of bank stocks and bonds. Appaloosa's investments in Citigroup and Bank of America generated substantial returns, underscoring Tepper's ability to profit from market dislocations by staying ahead of regulatory actions and capital flows.

Major Profits from Distressed Debt Investments: GM, Chrysler, and Others

In addition to his investments in the financial sector, Tepper's expertise in distressed debt led to significant gains from the automotive industry during the 2008 crisis. General Motors (GM) and Chrysler, two of the largest automakers in the United States, were on the brink of bankruptcy as consumer demand plummeted and credit markets froze.

Their distressed debt provided another ripe opportunity for Tepper's contrarian strategy. Tepper's analysis of GM and Chrysler centered on the potential for a government-backed restructuring rather than outright liquidation. He surmised that the government, facing political and economic pressure to preserve American jobs and manufacturing capabilities, would likely orchestrate a bailout or structured bankruptcy process to keep these companies operational. Appaloosa invested heavily in the distressed bonds of GM and Chrysler at steep discounts, with the belief that these bonds would recover value as the companies underwent restructuring. This investment required a detailed understanding of the restructuring process, the potential for asset recovery, and the likely terms of any government intervention.

Tepper's insight proved prescient when the government announced a structured bankruptcy for both automakers, coupled with financial support to facilitate their recovery. The restructuring plans allowed GM and Chrysler to emerge from bankruptcy with cleaner balance sheets and restructured operations, leading to a recovery in the value of their bonds. Appaloosa's investments in these distressed debts yielded substantial profits, demonstrating Tepper's ability to navigate complex corporate workouts and anticipate regulatory outcomes.

Beyond GM and Chrysler, Appaloosa also profited from other distressed debt investments during the financial crisis. The firm targeted companies in sectors such as real estate, airlines, and industrials, where market pessimism had driven bond prices to distressed levels. Tepper's team conducted thorough analyses to identify which companies had viable paths to recovery, leveraging their expertise to make informed investment decisions.

Other Significant Investments That Contributed to Appaloosa's Success

Appaloosa Management's success extended beyond the financial crisis, with several other notable investments contributing to its impressive track record. Tepper's ability to adapt his investment strategies to changing market conditions and sectors played a crucial role in the firm's ongoing achievements.

One significant investment was in the energy sector, particularly in companies like SunEdison and NRG Energy. As the renewable energy market began to grow, Tepper identified opportunities in the debt and equity of companies transitioning to clean energy. Despite initial volatility and challenges, Appaloosa's investments in this sector capitalized on the long-term growth potential of renewable energy and regulatory support for sustainable technologies.

Another notable area of investment was in airline debt. During periods of economic downturns or industry-specific crises, the airline industry often faced severe financial pressures, leading to distressed valuations of airline bonds. Tepper's approach involved acquiring these bonds at discounted prices and profiting from the eventual recovery in the airline industry as travel demand rebounded and companies restructured their operations.

Appaloosa also made strategic investments in the real estate sector, particularly in mortgage-backed securities and real estate investment trusts (REITs). Tepper's team focused on identifying undervalued securities in the aftermath of the housing market collapse and the subsequent recovery. By analyzing the underlying assets and market trends, Appaloosa was able to generate returns from the recovery in real estate values and the stabilization of mortgage markets. One of Tepper's key insights in these investments was the importance of understanding both macroeconomic trends and company-specific fundamentals. His ability to synthesize these factors allowed Appaloosa to make informed bets on sectors and securities that offered the potential for outsized returns, even in the face of market volatility.

Analysis of Tepper's Risk-Taking and Market Insights

David Tepper's success at Appaloosa Management is often attributed to his contrarian investment philosophy, but it is his nuanced approach to risk-taking and market insights that truly set him apart. Tepper's ability to identify and capitalize on distressed assets, coupled with his willingness to take calculated risks, has been central to Appaloosa's success.

Tepper's risk-taking strategy involves a meticulous evaluation of potential investments, focusing on both the upside potential and the inherent risks. His approach to distressed debt investing, for example, required a deep understanding of the restructuring process, creditor negotiations, and the potential for asset recovery. Tepper's willingness to invest in distressed assets was not driven by a blind appetite for risk, but rather by a rigorous analysis of the likelihood of recovery and the pricing of those risks in the market. Tepper's market insights are also rooted in his ability to anticipate macroeconomic trends and regulatory actions. His success during the 2008 financial crisis, for example, was largely due to his foresight in predicting government interventions and understanding how these actions would affect asset prices.

Tepper's ability to stay ahead of policy shifts and market dynamics allowed him to position Appaloosa's portfolio to benefit from impending changes. Furthermore, Tepper's approach to risk management involves maintaining flexibility and liquidity in his investments. By keeping a portion of Appaloosa's assets in cash or highly liquid securities, Tepper ensured that the firm could take advantage of sudden market opportunities or adjust its positions in response to changing conditions. This liquidity strategy was crucial during periods of market dislocation, allowing Appaloosa to deploy capital effectively when distressed assets became available at attractive prices. Tepper's contrarian approach is also characterized by his willingness to go against the prevailing market sentiment. While many investors were exiting positions during the financial crisis or other periods of uncertainty, Tepper's conviction in his analysis led him to increase his investments in distressed assets.

His ability to maintain this contrarian stance, even in the face of widespread pessimism, highlights his confidence in his investment thesis and his resilience in managing market pressures. Appaloosa Management's biggest wins under David Tepper's leadership exemplify the power of contrarian investing and the importance of rigorous risk management. Tepper's strategic investments during the 2008 financial crisis, including his successful bets on the debt and equity of major financial institutions and distressed automakers, showcased his ability to identify undervalued assets and anticipate regulatory interventions. Beyond the financial crisis, Appaloosa's success continued through strategic investments in sectors like energy, airlines, and real estate.

Tepper's willingness to take calculated risks, his deep market insights, and his disciplined approach to managing liquidity and flexibility have been central to the firm's ability to generate substantial returns for its investors. Tepper's legacy at Appaloosa Management is a testament to the effectiveness of contrarian strategies and the value of thorough analysis in navigating complex and volatile markets. His success demonstrates how a keen understanding of market dynamics, combined with a willingness to embrace risk and a contrarian mindset, can lead to remarkable investment achievements.

Appaloosa's biggest wins reflect Tepper's exceptional ability to turn market adversity into opportunity and his enduring impact on the hedge fund industry.

Chapter Five; Philanthropy and Ownership of Sports Teams

David Tepper's journey from hedge fund titan to philanthropist and sports team owner reflects a broadening of his ambitions beyond the financial markets. While his prowess in investment and risk management made him one of the wealthiest individuals in the world, Tepper has dedicated significant resources to philanthropy and sports, impacting communities, educational institutions, and professional sports landscapes.

This chapter explores Tepper's major philanthropic endeavors, his substantial contributions to Carnegie Mellon University and other organizations, and his strategic acquisition of the Carolina Panthers and launch of Charlotte FC. It delves into his motivations, the impact of his efforts, and his broader goals for community engagement through sports team ownership.

Tepper's Philanthropic Endeavors: Major Donations and Causes Supported

David Tepper's philanthropic journey is marked by a commitment to education, health, and community development. His philanthropy is characterized by substantial financial contributions and a focus on causes that create long-term impact and opportunities for advancement. Tepper's approach to giving reflects his belief in supporting initiatives that drive systemic change and benefit society at large.

One of Tepper's significant philanthropic focuses is education. He has made substantial donations to various educational institutions, aiming to enhance academic programs, facilities, and scholarship opportunities. Tepper's contributions have supported efforts to improve educational access and quality, particularly for underserved communities.

In 2013, Tepper donated $67 million to Carnegie Mellon University (CMU), his alma mater, to establish the David A. Tepper Quadrangle, a transformative project that included the construction of the Tepper School of Business's new home. This gift represented the largest donation in CMU's history and underscored Tepper's commitment to advancing business education.

The Tepper Quadrangle includes state-of-the-art classrooms, collaborative spaces, and facilities designed to foster innovation and interdisciplinary learning. Tepper's donation not only enhanced CMU's infrastructure but also provided resources for scholarships and faculty support, expanding opportunities for students and elevating the university's academic programs. Tepper's philanthropy also extends to healthcare. He has made significant contributions to hospitals and medical research institutions, supporting efforts to advance patient care and medical innovation. His donations have funded research initiatives, facility upgrades, and community health programs, reflecting his commitment to improving health outcomes and supporting medical advancements.

In addition to education and healthcare, Tepper's philanthropic efforts encompass social services and community development. He has supported organizations that address homelessness, food insecurity, and other social challenges, providing critical resources to help vulnerable populations. Tepper's philanthropy in these areas reflects his broader vision of creating a positive impact on communities and improving the quality of life for those in need.

Contributions to Carnegie Mellon University and Other Institutions

Carnegie Mellon University has been a primary beneficiary of David Tepper's philanthropy. His relationship with CMU, where he earned his MBA, has been instrumental in shaping his giving priorities. Tepper's contributions to CMU exemplify his commitment to supporting higher education and fostering innovation.

In addition to his transformative donation for the Tepper Quadrangle, Tepper has made other significant contributions to CMU. These include funding scholarships and endowments that support students from diverse backgrounds, enabling them to access high-quality education and pursue their academic and professional goals. Tepper's support for scholarships aligns with his belief in the power of education to drive social mobility and create opportunities for individuals to succeed.

Tepper's involvement with CMU extends beyond financial contributions. He has actively engaged with the university's leadership and students, providing mentorship and guidance to aspiring business leaders. His involvement in CMU's activities and initiatives reflects his dedication to giving back to the institution that played a pivotal role in his career development.

Tepper's philanthropic contributions also extend to other educational institutions and causes. He has supported initiatives at the University of Pittsburgh, where he completed his undergraduate studies, contributing to scholarship programs and academic development. His donations have helped enhance the university's educational offerings and support students in their academic pursuits.

Beyond higher education, Tepper has contributed to educational programs and organizations focused on K-12 education. His support for these initiatives aims to improve educational access and quality at all levels, addressing disparities in education and providing resources to underserved schools and communities.

Acquisition of the Carolina Panthers NFL Team: Motivations and Impact

David Tepper's acquisition of the Carolina Panthers in 2018 marked his entry into the world of professional sports ownership. The purchase of the NFL team for $2.275 billion made Tepper the sole owner and positioned him as one of the most influential figures in American football. Tepper's motivations for acquiring the Panthers extended beyond the financial investment, encompassing a broader vision for the team's success and its role in the community.

Tepper's decision to buy the Panthers was driven by his long-standing passion for sports and his belief in the potential for sports teams to create positive community impact. As a long-time football fan and former minority owner of the Pittsburgh Steelers, Tepper recognized the unique influence and reach of NFL teams. He saw the Panthers as a platform to not only compete at the highest level of professional football but also to engage with the Charlotte community and contribute to regional development.

Under Tepper's ownership, the Panthers have focused on building a competitive team while fostering a strong connection with fans and the community. Tepper has emphasized the importance of creating a winning culture, investing in player development, and enhancing the team's facilities. His commitment to excellence on the field is matched by his dedication to community engagement, with initiatives aimed at supporting local charities, youth programs, and economic development in the Charlotte area. Tepper's acquisition of the Panthers also brought a renewed focus on the team's long-term sustainability and growth. He has explored opportunities to enhance the fan experience, including stadium upgrades and technological innovations.

Tepper's vision for the Panthers encompasses both competitive success and a strong sense of community involvement, reflecting his broader goals as a sports team owner.

Launching Charlotte FC MLS Team: Vision and Objectives

David Tepper's expansion into Major League Soccer (MLS) with the launch of Charlotte FC in 2019 demonstrated his commitment to diversifying his sports investments and supporting the growth of soccer in the United States. The creation of Charlotte FC as an expansion team in MLS was driven by Tepper's vision of establishing a successful franchise that could capture the enthusiasm for soccer in the region and contribute to the sport's development.

Tepper's decision to bring an MLS team to Charlotte was influenced by several factors, including the city's growing interest in soccer, its vibrant demographic composition, and the potential for soccer to unite diverse communities. He recognized the opportunity to build a soccer culture in Charlotte that would resonate with fans and provide a new avenue for sports engagement in the city.

The launch of Charlotte FC involved significant investments in infrastructure, including the renovation of Bank of America Stadium to accommodate soccer matches and the development of a training facility for the team. Tepper's commitment to creating a top-tier soccer club extended to assembling a competitive roster and hiring experienced management to guide the team's development.

His focus on establishing a strong foundation for Charlotte FC aimed to position the club for success both on and off the field. Tepper's objectives for Charlotte FC include fostering a strong fan base, creating an inclusive and engaging matchday experience, and contributing to the growth of soccer in the region. He has emphasized the importance of community involvement, with initiatives to connect with local schools, youth soccer programs, and community organizations.

Tepper's vision for Charlotte FC reflects his broader goals of using sports as a platform to create positive social and economic impact.

Tepper's Broader Goals with Sports Team Ownership and Community Engagement

David Tepper's ownership of sports teams, including the Carolina Panthers and Charlotte FC, is driven by a vision that extends beyond the traditional metrics of success in professional sports. His broader goals encompass community engagement, economic development, and creating opportunities for social impact through sports.

Tepper views sports teams as powerful vehicles for community connection and development. His approach to team ownership emphasizes the role of sports in bringing people together, fostering a sense of pride, and contributing to the social fabric of the community. Tepper's investments in the Panthers and Charlotte FC are accompanied by efforts to support local charities, educational programs, and economic initiatives, reflecting his commitment to giving back to the communities that support his teams. One of Tepper's key initiatives has been the creation of the David Tepper Charitable Foundation, which focuses on addressing social issues such as homelessness, education, and community development.

The foundation has supported a range of projects and organizations, including efforts to provide housing for homeless individuals, educational scholarships, and funding for community health programs. Tepper's philanthropy through the foundation aligns with his vision of using his resources and influence to create meaningful change. Tepper's broader goals also include leveraging the economic impact of his sports teams to drive regional development. He has explored opportunities to invest in infrastructure projects, such as stadium improvements and surrounding developments, that can stimulate local economies and create jobs. Tepper's vision for economic development through sports reflects his understanding of the potential for sports teams to contribute to urban revitalization and economic growth.

Additionally, Tepper's approach to team ownership involves a focus on innovation and forward-thinking strategies. He has emphasized the importance of embracing new technologies, data analytics, and fan engagement tools to enhance the performance and reach of his teams. Tepper's commitment to innovation is evident in his efforts to modernize the Panthers' operations and establish Charlotte FC as a competitive and technologically advanced soccer club. Tepper's involvement in professional sports also includes a commitment to diversity and inclusion. He has advocated for creating opportunities for underrepresented groups within his organizations and the broader sports industry.

Tepper's efforts to promote diversity extend to hiring practices, community outreach, and supporting initiatives that advance equity and inclusion in sports.

David Tepper's philanthropic endeavors and ownership of sports teams represent a significant expansion of his influence and impact beyond the financial world. His substantial contributions to education, healthcare, and community development reflect a commitment to creating positive social change and fostering opportunities for individuals and communities to thrive. Tepper's investments in the Carolina Panthers and Charlotte FC illustrate his broader vision of using sports as a catalyst for community engagement, economic development, and social impact.

Enhancing Community Engagement Through Sports

Tepper's approach to sports team ownership is deeply rooted in the belief that professional sports can play a transformative role in community engagement and cohesion. The Carolina Panthers and Charlotte FC have become more than just sports teams under his stewardship; they are central to his strategy for building stronger community ties and creating inclusive environments where fans and residents feel connected and valued.

For the Carolina Panthers, Tepper's initiatives have focused on enhancing fan experiences and deepening the team's community involvement. Recognizing the passionate support of Panthers fans, Tepper has invested in upgrading Bank of America Stadium to improve accessibility, comfort, and engagement during games. These enhancements include state-of-the-art video boards, better seating options, and upgraded amenities that contribute to a more immersive and enjoyable game-day atmosphere. Moreover, Tepper has championed community outreach programs that involve the Panthers in various charitable activities and local initiatives.

These programs include youth football camps, educational partnerships, and health and wellness events that leverage the team's influence to support and uplift the local community. The Panthers' involvement in such initiatives helps to foster a sense of belonging and pride among fans and residents, aligning with Tepper's vision of using sports as a tool for social good. Charlotte FC, as a newer addition to Tepper's sports portfolio, has similarly embraced a community-centric approach. Tepper's vision for the soccer club includes creating an inclusive and vibrant soccer culture in Charlotte, one that resonates with diverse groups and encourages widespread participation.

Charlotte FC has actively engaged with local soccer enthusiasts, schools, and youth organizations to promote the sport and develop grassroots programs that nurture young talent and foster a love for soccer.

The launch of Charlotte FC has been accompanied by community events and initiatives designed to build a loyal and enthusiastic fan base. These efforts include open training sessions, fan meet-and-greets, and collaborations with local businesses and organizations. Tepper's commitment to community engagement through Charlotte FC highlights his belief in the unifying power of sports and his desire to create a lasting and positive impact on the city of Charlotte.

Driving Economic Development Through Sports Investments

David Tepper's investments in the Carolina Panthers and Charlotte FC also reflect a strategic focus on driving economic development in the regions where these teams are based. By leveraging the economic potential of sports, Tepper aims to stimulate local economies, create jobs, and foster urban revitalization.

One of Tepper's key initiatives for the Panthers involves exploring the potential for developing a new stadium complex or enhancing the existing facilities to serve as a multi-use venue. Such a development could include commercial spaces, hotels, and entertainment venues that generate economic activity and create opportunities for local businesses. Tepper envisions these developments as catalysts for regional growth, attracting visitors and boosting the local economy through increased tourism, retail, and hospitality spending.

For Charlotte FC, Tepper's vision includes developing a state-of-the-art training facility and soccer-specific stadium that not only meets the team's needs but also serves as a community asset. This facility is intended to host a range of events, from youth soccer tournaments to concerts and other entertainment activities, providing additional revenue streams and supporting local economic development.

Tepper's investment in such infrastructure projects demonstrates his commitment to creating sustainable economic benefits for the region. Furthermore, Tepper's approach to economic development through sports extends to his engagement with local government and business leaders. He has actively participated in discussions about regional planning and development, advocating for investments in infrastructure and initiatives that support the growth of the sports and entertainment sectors.

Tepper's involvement in these efforts reflects his understanding of the broader economic impact of sports teams and his desire to contribute to the long-term prosperity of the communities where his teams operate.

Promoting Diversity and Inclusion in Sports

David Tepper's tenure as a sports team owner has been marked by a strong commitment to promoting diversity and inclusion within his organizations and the broader sports industry. Tepper recognizes the importance of creating inclusive environments that reflect the diversity of the communities his teams serve and provide opportunities for individuals from all backgrounds to succeed.

Within the Carolina Panthers and Charlotte FC, Tepper has implemented policies and practices aimed at fostering diversity and inclusion in hiring, team operations, and community outreach. This includes initiatives to increase representation of women and minorities in leadership roles, coaching positions, and front-office staff. Tepper's focus on diversity extends to creating inclusive fan experiences that welcome and celebrate fans from all walks of life. In addition to internal policies, Tepper has supported initiatives that address broader issues of equity and social justice. Both the Panthers and Charlotte FC have been involved in campaigns and programs that promote equality, combat discrimination, and support marginalized communities.

These efforts include partnerships with local organizations that advocate for social justice, as well as team-driven initiatives that raise awareness and funds for causes related to diversity and inclusion. Tepper's commitment to diversity and inclusion is also evident in his approach to team culture and player development. He has emphasized the importance of creating a positive and supportive environment for players, where diversity is valued and everyone has the opportunity to contribute and excel.
Tepper's focus on fostering an inclusive culture helps to attract and retain top talent,

both on and off the field, and aligns with his broader goals of using sports to drive positive social change.

Long-Term Vision and Impact of Tepper's Philanthropy and Sports Investments

David Tepper's philanthropic endeavors and sports investments are driven by a long-term vision of creating meaningful and lasting impact. His approach to giving and team ownership reflects a strategic focus on sustainability, innovation, and community engagement, with the goal of leaving a positive legacy that extends beyond financial success.

Tepper's philanthropy is characterized by a commitment to supporting initiatives that create long-term value and address systemic challenges. His substantial donations to educational institutions, healthcare, and social services are designed to provide enduring benefits and empower individuals and communities to achieve their potential. Tepper's emphasis on education, in particular, highlights his belief in the transformative power of learning and the importance of providing opportunities for future generations. In the realm of sports, Tepper's investments in the Panthers and Charlotte FC reflect his vision of building successful and socially responsible organizations that contribute to the well-being of their communities. His focus on enhancing fan experiences, fostering community engagement, and driving economic development aligns with his broader goals of using sports as a platform for positive impact.

Tepper's commitment to diversity and inclusion further underscores his desire to create equitable and inclusive environments within his teams and the sports industry as a whole. Tepper's long-term vision for his sports investments also includes a focus on innovation and adaptability. He has embraced new technologies and data-driven approaches to enhance team performance, fan engagement, and operational efficiency.

Tepper's willingness to invest in cutting-edge solutions and explore new opportunities reflects his forward-thinking approach to sports team ownership and his desire to position his teams for sustained success in a rapidly evolving landscape. Overall, David Tepper's philanthropic efforts and sports team ownership represent a multifaceted strategy for creating positive change and leveraging his resources for the greater good. His contributions to education, healthcare, and community development, combined with his investments in professional sports, reflect a holistic approach to giving and leadership that aims to make a lasting and meaningful impact on society.

Tepper's legacy as a philanthropist and sports team owner is defined by his commitment to excellence, innovation, and community engagement, demonstrating how individuals can use their influence and wealth to drive positive social and economic outcomes.

Chapter Six; Tepper's Leadership and Management Style

David Tepper's rise as a hedge fund titan and influential leader in the financial world is marked by a distinctive management style and leadership approach that have set him apart from his peers. Known for his unconventional methods, keen decision-making processes, and emphasis on talent and risk-taking, Tepper has created a reputation as a formidable and innovative leader.

This chapter delves into the core aspects of Tepper's leadership qualities, his unorthodox business practices, his focus on leveraging talent over traditional experience, and insights from those who have worked closely with him.

Analysis of Tepper's Leadership Qualities and Decision-Making Processes

David Tepper's leadership style is characterized by a blend of decisiveness, adaptability, and a willingness to embrace risk. These qualities have been instrumental in his success as the founder and leader of Appaloosa Management and as an owner of professional sports teams.

Tepper's ability to navigate complex financial landscapes and make bold investment decisions has earned him recognition as one of the most astute and successful investors of his generation. At the heart of Tepper's decision-making process is a profound analytical ability and a deep understanding of market dynamics. Tepper is known for his meticulous approach to analyzing market trends, company financials, and economic indicators.

This rigorous analysis allows him to identify undervalued assets and opportunities that others might overlook. Tepper's investment decisions are often grounded in thorough research and a clear understanding of the potential risks and rewards.

Tepper's decisiveness is another hallmark of his leadership. Once he has identified a promising investment opportunity, he acts swiftly and with conviction. This decisiveness has enabled him to capitalize on market dislocations and make significant returns during periods of economic turmoil. For example, during the 2008 financial crisis, Tepper's bold bets on distressed financial assets and his confidence in the eventual recovery of the markets led to substantial gains for Appaloosa Management. His ability to act decisively in times of uncertainty has been a key driver of his success.

Adaptability is also a critical component of Tepper's leadership style. He has demonstrated a capacity to adjust his strategies in response to changing market conditions and emerging trends. Tepper's willingness to adapt is evident in his ability to navigate various market environments and invest in a diverse range of assets, from equities to distressed debt.

This flexibility allows him to seize opportunities across different sectors and geographies, positioning Appaloosa Management to thrive in dynamic and evolving markets. Tepper's leadership is further characterized by a strong focus on resilience and risk management. He recognizes the importance of managing downside risk and protecting his investments from potential losses.

Tepper's approach to risk management involves rigorous stress testing of investment scenarios and maintaining a balanced portfolio that can weather market volatility. His emphasis on resilience ensures that Appaloosa Management can sustain its performance even during challenging economic periods.

Unconventional Methods: Examples of His Unorthodox Approach to Business

David Tepper's success can be attributed in part to his unconventional and unorthodox approach to business. His methods often defy traditional norms and practices in the financial industry, setting him apart as a maverick investor willing to challenge the status quo.

One of Tepper's notable unconventional practices is his contrarian investment strategy. While many investors follow market trends and herd mentality, Tepper is known for taking positions that run counter to prevailing market sentiments. He often invests in distressed or undervalued assets that others have abandoned, betting on their recovery and long-term potential. This contrarian approach was evident during the 2008 financial crisis, when Tepper made significant investments in distressed financial institutions and assets, despite widespread pessimism about their prospects. His ability to identify value where others see only risk has been a defining feature of his investment philosophy.

Another example of Tepper's unorthodox methods is his willingness to engage directly with the management teams of the companies in which he invests. Unlike many investors who remain passive, Tepper actively involves himself in the strategic decisions and turnaround efforts of his portfolio companies. His hands-on approach allows him to influence key decisions, drive operational improvements, and align company strategies with his investment objectives. This active engagement has been instrumental in turning around struggling companies and creating value for Appaloosa Management's investments.

Tepper's approach to team building and management is also unconventional. He places a strong emphasis on assembling a team of exceptionally talented and intelligent individuals, often prioritizing raw talent and potential over traditional experience and credentials. Tepper's hiring practices reflect his belief that intelligence and creativity are more important than conventional industry experience.

He seeks out individuals who can bring fresh perspectives and innovative ideas to the table, fostering a culture of intellectual rigor and dynamic problem-solving within Appaloosa Management. In addition, Tepper's leadership style is characterized by a high level of transparency and openness with his team. He encourages open communication, candid feedback, and a collaborative approach to decision-making. This transparency extends to sharing the firm's strategies, performance metrics, and investment rationale with his team, ensuring that everyone is aligned and informed. Tepper's open-door policy and willingness to listen to diverse viewpoints contribute to a culture of trust and accountability, empowering his team to take ownership of their work and contribute to the firm's success.

Focus on Talent, Intelligence, and Risk-Taking Over Traditional Experience

David Tepper's approach to building and leading his team is grounded in a focus on talent, intelligence, and risk-taking, rather than adhering strictly to traditional experience and qualifications. This focus has allowed him to cultivate a dynamic and innovative team at Appaloosa Management that can navigate complex investment challenges and seize opportunities in the market.

Tepper's emphasis on talent is evident in his recruitment and hiring practices. He seeks out individuals with exceptional analytical abilities, creative thinking skills, and a strong aptitude for understanding complex financial concepts. Tepper values intellectual curiosity and the ability to think critically, often hiring people who may not have extensive industry experience but demonstrate strong potential and a willingness to learn. This approach enables Appaloosa Management to attract diverse talent with unique perspectives and ideas, fostering a culture of continuous learning and innovation.

Intelligence is another key attribute that Tepper prioritizes in his team members. He believes that having a team of highly intelligent individuals allows the firm to tackle complex investment problems and develop sophisticated strategies. Tepper encourages his team to engage in rigorous analysis, question assumptions, and explore new investment opportunities with a critical eye. This emphasis on intelligence ensures that Appaloosa Management remains at the forefront of financial innovation and can adapt to evolving market conditions.

Risk-taking is a central component of Tepper's leadership philosophy. He encourages his team to embrace calculated risks and pursue bold investment opportunities that have the potential to generate substantial returns. Tepper's own track record of making contrarian bets and investing in distressed assets serves as a model for his team, inspiring them to think outside the box and challenge conventional wisdom.

By fostering a culture that values risk-taking and rewards innovative thinking, Tepper empowers his team to pursue unconventional strategies and capitalize on market inefficiencies. Tepper's focus on talent, intelligence, and risk-taking extends to his approach to professional development and team dynamics. He provides opportunities for his team members to take on significant responsibilities, lead investment initiatives, and contribute to the firm's strategic direction.

Tepper's mentorship and support help his team members develop their skills and grow as leaders within the firm, creating a pipeline of talent that can drive Appaloosa Management's continued success.

Insights from Colleagues and Employees on Working with Tepper

David Tepper's colleagues and employees offer valuable insights into his leadership style and the experience of working with him. Their perspectives highlight Tepper's effectiveness as a leader, his commitment to excellence, and his impact on the culture and performance of Appaloosa Management.

Colleagues describe Tepper as a leader who combines deep expertise with a genuine passion for investing. His enthusiasm for financial markets and his hands-on approach to managing the firm inspire those around him to strive for excellence. Tepper's colleagues appreciate his ability to stay deeply involved in the firm's operations and investment decisions, while also providing strategic guidance and support. His leadership style is characterized by a balance of direct involvement and delegation, allowing team members to take initiative and contribute meaningfully to the firm's success. Employees of Appaloosa Management frequently highlight Tepper's commitment to fostering a collaborative and intellectually stimulating work environment. They describe him as approachable and willing to engage in open discussions about investment strategies and market trends.

Tepper's willingness to listen to diverse viewpoints and encourage debate creates a culture of intellectual rigor and innovation. Employees feel empowered to share their ideas and contribute to the firm's investment decisions, knowing that their insights are valued and considered. Tepper's focus on talent and intelligence is also reflected in the feedback from his team. Employees describe him as someone who recognizes and nurtures potential, providing opportunities for growth and professional development. Tepper's mentorship and support are seen as critical to the success of

Appaloosa Management's team members, helping them build their skills and advance their careers. His emphasis on hiring based on potential rather than traditional experience allows the firm to attract and retain top talent with diverse backgrounds and perspectives.

In terms of Tepper's management style, employees appreciate his transparency and straightforward communication. Tepper is known for being direct and candid in his feedback, providing clear guidance and expectations. This approach helps create a culture of accountability and performance, where team members understand their roles and responsibilities and are motivated to deliver results. Tepper's clear and honest communication style fosters trust and alignment within the team, contributing to a cohesive and effective organizational culture.

Overall, the insights from Tepper's colleagues and employees underscore his effectiveness as a leader who combines deep financial expertise with a commitment to fostering a dynamic and innovative work environment. His focus on talent, intelligence, and risk-taking, along with his unconventional approach to business, has positioned Appaloosa Management as a leading hedge fund with a strong track record of success.

David Tepper's leadership and management style are defined by his decisive decision-making, adaptability, and a willingness to challenge conventional norms. His emphasis on talent, intelligence, and risk-taking over traditional experience has shaped the culture and success of Appaloosa Management, making it a standout in the competitive hedge fund industry.

Driving Innovation and Success at Appaloosa Management

Tepper's leadership at Appaloosa Management reflects a continuous drive for innovation and success. He has cultivated an environment where questioning assumptions and exploring new ideas are not just encouraged but expected. This innovative mindset has allowed Appaloosa to stay ahead of market trends and adapt to changing financial landscapes.

One key aspect of Tepper's approach is his openness to unconventional investment strategies. Unlike many traditional hedge funds that might rely on established methodologies, Tepper encourages his team to think creatively and pursue unique investment opportunities. This has included investing in distressed debt during economic downturns and making bold contrarian bets that others might shy away from. By fostering a culture that values creativity and innovation, Tepper ensures that Appaloosa remains agile and able to capitalize on emerging opportunities. Tepper's commitment to innovation is also evident in his adoption of technology and data analytics.

He recognizes the importance of leveraging advanced tools and techniques to gain insights into market trends and enhance investment decisions. Appaloosa Management employs sophisticated data analysis to identify patterns, assess risks, and optimize portfolio performance. Tepper's willingness to invest in technology and embrace data-driven decision-making has given Appaloosa a competitive edge in the hedge fund industry.

Building a Culture of Excellence and Accountability

Under Tepper's leadership, Appaloosa Management has developed a culture of excellence and accountability that permeates all aspects of the firm's operations. This culture is grounded in a strong work ethic, a commitment to high standards, and a focus on delivering results.

Tepper sets the tone for excellence through his own dedication and work ethic. He is known for being deeply involved in the firm's day-to-day activities, from analyzing investment opportunities to mentoring team members. Tepper's hands-on approach and attention to detail demonstrate his commitment to maintaining the highest standards of performance. His leadership inspires his team to strive for excellence and take pride in their work.

Accountability is another cornerstone of Appaloosa's culture. Tepper expects his team members to take ownership of their responsibilities and be accountable for their decisions and actions.

This accountability extends to all levels of the organization, from junior analysts to senior managers. Tepper's emphasis on accountability ensures that everyone at Appaloosa is aligned with the firm's goals and committed to achieving its objectives. It also fosters a culture of trust and transparency, where team members are encouraged to learn from their mistakes and continuously improve.

Empowering and Developing Talent

Tepper's focus on talent and intelligence over traditional experience has resulted in a dynamic and diverse team at Appaloosa Management. He recognizes that nurturing and developing talent is essential to the firm's long-term success, and he invests in creating opportunities for his team members to grow and excel.

Professional development is a priority at Appaloosa, with Tepper providing access to training, mentorship, and resources that support career growth. He encourages team members to take on challenging projects, lead initiatives, and expand their skill sets. Tepper's mentorship is particularly valued, as he shares his insights, provides guidance, and helps his team navigate complex investment decisions. This support fosters a collaborative learning environment where team members feel empowered to take risks and pursue innovative ideas.

Tepper also promotes a culture of recognition and reward, where outstanding performance is acknowledged and celebrated. High-performing individuals are given opportunities for advancement and increased responsibilities, reinforcing the firm's commitment to recognizing and cultivating talent. This approach not only motivates team members to excel but also helps Appaloosa attract and retain top talent in a competitive industry.

Insights from Tepper's Broader Influence

David Tepper's leadership and management style extend beyond Appaloosa Management to his other ventures, including his ownership of the Carolina Panthers and Charlotte FC. His approach to leading these organizations reflects many of the same principles that have driven his success in finance: a focus on talent, a commitment to innovation, and a willingness to embrace risk. In his role as a sports team owner, Tepper has applied his business acumen and leadership skills to drive performance and foster community engagement. He has invested in enhancing fan experiences, developing team facilities, and supporting community outreach initiatives.

Tepper's leadership in sports demonstrates his ability to translate his management principles to different contexts, leveraging his expertise to create value and drive positive outcomes. Tepper's broader influence also includes his philanthropic efforts, where he applies the same strategic and impactful approach. His contributions to education, healthcare, and social services reflect his commitment to making a meaningful difference and addressing systemic challenges. Tepper's philanthropy is characterized by a focus on long-term impact, sustainability, and empowerment, mirroring his approach to leadership and management in his professional ventures. David Tepper's leadership and management style have been instrumental in shaping the success of Appaloosa Management and his broader ventures. His decisive decision-making, adaptability, and willingness to embrace risk have enabled him to navigate complex financial landscapes and seize opportunities that others might overlook.

Tepper's emphasis on talent, intelligence, and risk-taking over traditional experience has fostered a dynamic and innovative culture at Appaloosa, driving the firm's success and positioning it as a leader in the hedge fund industry. Tepper's unorthodox methods, such as his contrarian investment strategy and hands-on involvement with portfolio companies, have set him apart as a maverick investor willing to challenge conventional norms. His focus on building a culture of excellence, accountability, and continuous improvement has created an environment where team members are empowered to take risks, innovate, and excel. The insights from Tepper's colleagues and employees highlight his effectiveness as a leader who combines deep financial expertise with a commitment to fostering a collaborative and intellectually stimulating work environment.

His open communication, transparent leadership, and support for professional development have contributed to a cohesive and high-performing team at Appaloosa. Beyond his success in finance, Tepper's broader influence in sports team ownership and philanthropy demonstrates his ability to apply his leadership principles to different contexts and drive positive impact. His investments in professional sports and his strategic philanthropic efforts reflect his vision of using his resources and expertise to create value, drive economic development, and support communities.

In summary, David Tepper's leadership and management style are defined by a unique combination of decisiveness, adaptability, and a focus on talent and innovation. His unconventional approach to business, commitment to excellence, and ability to empower his team have been key drivers of his success and have established him as a leading figure in the financial industry and beyond. Tepper's legacy as a leader is characterized by his ability to navigate uncertainty, embrace risk, and leverage his influence to create lasting and meaningful impact.

Chapter Seven; Tepper's Wealth and Lifestyle

David Tepper, the billionaire founder of Appaloosa Management, is renowned for his acumen in finance and investment. His journey from a modest background to amassing a staggering fortune has placed him among the global elite. Tepper's wealth, estimated to be around $20 billion, reflects his success and strategic prowess in the hedge fund industry. Yet, despite his vast riches, Tepper's lifestyle and public persona are marked by a unique blend of affluence and unpretentiousness.

Overview of Tepper's Net Worth and Standing Among Global Billionaires

David Tepper's net worth is a testament to his exceptional skills in identifying and capitalizing on investment opportunities. His ability to navigate financial markets, particularly during times of economic distress, has earned him significant profits and solidified his reputation as a leading hedge fund manager. With an estimated fortune that places him in the upper echelons of global billionaires, Tepper's wealth is reflective of his remarkable career achievements.

Tepper's standing among the world's richest individuals is bolstered by his consistent performance in managing Appaloosa Management, a hedge fund known for its high returns and strategic investments. His fortune peaked during the aftermath of the 2008 financial crisis, where his contrarian investments in distressed assets yielded substantial gains. This period showcased Tepper's ability to identify value where others saw risk, a characteristic that has defined his career and contributed to his significant net worth.

According to Forbes and Bloomberg's billionaire rankings, Tepper has often been listed among the top wealthiest individuals globally. His position fluctuates slightly with market conditions and investment outcomes, but he remains a prominent figure in the financial world. Tepper's inclusion in these rankings underscores his financial influence and the success of his investment strategies.

Tepper's wealth is not just a reflection of his business acumen but also of his strategic diversification into various asset classes. Beyond hedge fund management, he has made substantial personal investments in real estate, fine art, and other high-value assets, further augmenting his net worth. These investments provide a glimpse into Tepper's approach to wealth management, emphasizing diversification and long-term value creation.

Tepper's Personal Investments in Real Estate, Cars, and Art

David Tepper's personal investments extend beyond the financial markets, showcasing his interest in real estate, luxury cars, and fine art. These investments reflect his appreciation for tangible assets and his strategic approach to building and maintaining wealth.

Real Estate

Tepper's real estate portfolio is a significant component of his personal wealth, featuring high-end properties in some of the most desirable locations. One of his most notable acquisitions is his estate in the Hamptons, a luxurious beachfront property that exemplifies opulence. Purchased for a substantial sum, this estate includes expansive living spaces, stunning views, and state-of-the-art amenities, underscoring Tepper's preference for properties that combine comfort with investment potential. In addition to his Hamptons estate, Tepper owns a penthouse in Miami Beach, known for its panoramic ocean views and prime location. This property aligns with his lifestyle, offering both luxury and convenience.

Tepper's real estate investments also include properties in his home state of New Jersey, further diversifying his holdings and providing a mix of leisure and practicality. Tepper's approach to real estate is indicative of his broader investment philosophy: he seeks properties that not only offer personal enjoyment but also possess significant appreciation potential. This strategy ensures that his real estate holdings contribute to his overall wealth while providing him with high-quality living environments.

Cars

Tepper's collection of luxury cars reflects his penchant for high-performance vehicles and sophisticated engineering. His fleet includes prestigious brands such as Ferrari, Porsche, and Mercedes-Benz, each selected for their performance, design, and prestige. These vehicles are more than just modes of transportation; they are symbols of Tepper's success and his appreciation for the craftsmanship and innovation that these brands represent.

Among his collection is a Ferrari 488 GTB, known for its speed and aesthetic appeal. This car, like others in his garage, represents the intersection of luxury and performance, embodying the qualities Tepper values in his personal investments. His interest in cars also highlights his willingness to indulge in his passions, balancing his professional achievements with personal enjoyment.

Art

Tepper's investments in fine art reflect his cultural interests and his appreciation for aesthetic value. His art collection includes works by renowned artists, adding a layer of sophistication and cultural engagement to his portfolio. Tepper's approach to art collection is not just about acquiring valuable pieces but also about supporting the arts and enjoying the cultural enrichment that comes with owning significant artworks.

His collection includes pieces from various periods and styles, ranging from classic to contemporary art. This diversity mirrors Tepper's broader investment strategy, emphasizing a balanced approach that includes both traditional and modern assets. By investing in art, Tepper not only diversifies his portfolio but also aligns his financial interests with his personal passions.

Reflection on Tepper's Lifestyle Choices and Public Image as a "Regular Guy"

Despite his immense wealth and high-profile investments, David Tepper is often described as embodying the persona of a "regular guy." This image is shaped by his down-to-earth demeanor, straightforward communication style, and his efforts to maintain a sense of normalcy despite his billionaire status.

Tepper's lifestyle choices reflect a balance between enjoying the luxuries afforded by his wealth and retaining a grounded, approachable image. For instance, while he owns multimillion-dollar properties and a fleet of luxury cars, he is also known for his straightforward and unpretentious demeanor. Colleagues and acquaintances often describe him as approachable, pragmatic, and relatable, qualities that contribute to his public image as a regular individual who has achieved extraordinary success. One aspect of Tepper's lifestyle that reinforces this image is his involvement in community and philanthropic activities. He is known for his significant charitable contributions, particularly in the areas of education and healthcare.

Tepper's philanthropy is marked by a strategic approach that aims to create lasting impact rather than merely providing financial support. His donations to institutions like Carnegie Mellon University and various healthcare organizations reflect his commitment to giving back and making a positive difference in society. Tepper's philanthropic efforts also include support for local initiatives and causes that resonate with his personal values.

By investing in community development and educational opportunities, Tepper demonstrates his desire to use his wealth for the greater good, aligning his public persona with his actions.

Moreover, Tepper's personal interactions and communication style further solidify his image as a regular guy. He is known for his candid and straightforward manner, whether in business settings or public appearances. Tepper's ability to connect with people on a personal level, coupled with his willingness to share his insights and experiences, contributes to his relatable image. In his public appearances and interviews, Tepper often emphasizes his humble beginnings and the values that have guided his success. He speaks candidly about the challenges he faced early in his career and the lessons he learned along the way.

This openness about his journey, combined with his willingness to share advice and insights, makes him relatable to a broad audience and enhances his reputation as a self-made billionaire who has not lost touch with his roots.

Tepper's lifestyle also includes elements of simplicity and normalcy, such as his interest in sports and his engagement with his local community. His ownership of the Carolina Panthers and Charlotte FC, for instance, reflects his passion for sports and his desire to contribute to the local community through his investments. Tepper's involvement in these teams goes beyond financial interest; it demonstrates his commitment to fostering local sports culture and providing opportunities for community engagement.

David Tepper's wealth and lifestyle present a multifaceted picture of a man who has achieved extraordinary financial success while maintaining a grounded and relatable public image. His substantial net worth, bolstered by his successful hedge fund management and strategic personal investments, places him among the world's most influential billionaires.

Yet, despite his vast riches, Tepper's lifestyle choices and public persona reflect a balance between enjoying the luxuries of wealth and maintaining a sense of normalcy. Tepper's investments in real estate, luxury cars, and fine art illustrate his appreciation for high-quality assets and his strategic approach to wealth management. His properties, cars, and art collection are not only symbols of his success but also reflect his personal tastes and interests. These investments contribute to his overall wealth while providing him with enjoyment and cultural enrichment.

Tepper's public image as a regular guy is reinforced by his down-to-earth demeanor, his straightforward communication style, and his commitment to philanthropy. His significant charitable contributions, particularly in education and healthcare, demonstrate his desire to use his wealth for positive impact and community development.

Tepper's involvement in sports team ownership further showcases his passion for sports and his engagement with his local community. In summary, David Tepper's wealth and lifestyle embody a unique blend of affluence and approachability. His financial success, personal investments, and philanthropic efforts reflect his strategic acumen and his commitment to making a positive difference.

Despite his billionaire status, Tepper's relatable persona and down-to-earth approach continue to define his public image, making him a distinctive and influential figure in both the financial world and broader society.

Conclusion

As we reach the end of this captivating odyssey, it's clear that David Tepper's story is one of extraordinary transformation - a testament to the power of grit, intelligence, and unconventional thinking. From his humble beginnings in the steel city of Pittsburgh to his current status as a billionaire hedge fund titan and sports team owner, Tepper's journey is a true embodiment of the American dream.

The key lessons we can draw from Tepper's life and career are manifold. His relentless pursuit of knowledge, his willingness to take calculated risks, and his ability to identify undervalued opportunities have all been instrumental to his remarkable success. Equally inspiring is Tepper's resilience in the face of adversity - his capacity to bounce back from setbacks and adapt his strategies to changing market conditions.

But Tepper's legacy extends far beyond the realm of finance. His philanthropic efforts, including his $67 million donation to

Carnegie Mellon University, have had a profound impact on the lives of countless individuals. And his recent forays into sports team ownership, with the acquisition of the Carolina Panthers and Charlotte FC, showcase his desire to leave a lasting mark on the world of athletics as well.

As Tepper continues to shape the future, his influence is likely to extend even further. His unconventional approach to business and his willingness to challenge the status quo have the potential to inspire a new generation of entrepreneurs and investors. Moreover, his commitment to giving back and his passion for sports could pave the way for innovative partnerships and initiatives that positively impact communities around the world. In the end, David Tepper's story is a testament to the transformative power of the human spirit. His journey from a middle-class upbringing to the pinnacles of wealth and influence is a captivating tale that will continue to inspire and enlighten readers for generations to come. Thank you for joining us on this remarkable odyssey - we hope that Tepper's story has left an indelible mark on your own aspirations and dreams.

Made in United States
North Haven, CT
18 July 2025

70817146R00085